THE OFFICIAL  SPORT
FORMULAONE
ANNUAL 2009

Written by David Clayton
Designed by Simon Thorley

A Grange Publication

© 2008. Published by Grange Communications Ltd., Edinburgh, under licence from Granada Ventures Ltd. Printed in the EU.

Photographs © Action Images / Reuters

ISBN 978-1-906211-33-2

£6.99

CONTENTS

F1 CHAMPIONSHIP REVIEW 2007

It was the closest ever finish to the Formula One Drivers' Championship

Prior to the final race of the season, Lewis Hamilton appeared to be in pole position, poised to become the first rookie to win the title at the first attempt. Few would have argued that Hamilton wouldn't have been a worthy winner, but a series of unfortunate events in the remaining weeks of the 2007 F1 season saw the young British driver foiled by the narrowest of margins.

Finland's Kimi Räikkönen had never been far from the top of the leader's board, but he needed a lot of luck and a faultless last race in order to vault ahead of Hamilton and Fernando Alonso – and that's exactly what he got. He won the title by a single point ahead of Hamilton and Alonso who tied for second with 109 points. Though many believed Hamilton's verve and daring style of driving made him the best driver to watch, Räikkönen refused to believe his chance had gone and with a strong finish he came from nowhere to claim a remarkable victory.

It was Räikkönen who won the opening race of the season, taking the Australian Grand Prix, but he failed to win his next six races as Felipe Massa, Alonso and Hamilton swapped the podium positions between themselves, each winning twice. Lewis Hamilton won his first Grand Prix in Canada and followed it up by winning a second consecutive race in the USA. Though Räikkönen returned to winning ways by winning the next two Grands Prix, Hamilton finished in third each time meaning he'd finished on the podium in his first nine races – an incredible feat for a rookie driver. Both Räikkönen and Hamilton then finished out of the points in the European Grand Prix, allowing Alonso back in the title hunt, but with seven races to go, everything began to go right for Räikkönen – and everything that could go wrong for Hamilton, did go wrong. The Finn would never finish outside of the top three again, while Hamilton managed just three podium finishes.

With two races to go, it seemed to be between McLaren team-mates Alonso and Hamilton and for the penultimate race of the season in China, Hamilton, twelve points clear at the top of the Drivers' Championship, started on pole position, knowing a win or a finish within one point of Alonso would guarantee the title. But the weather conspired against him and he became stuck in gravel on lap 30, ending his challenge. Räikkönen went on to win the race with Alonso finishing second meaning that all three drivers were still in with a chance of the title going into the last Grand Prix of the season in Brazil. Hamilton encountered gear-box problems early in the race and though he recovered slightly in the latter stages, Räikkönen gave a faultless performance to win the race and with Alonso finishing third, it meant the title went back to Finland, not Spain or the UK. No doubt Lewis Hamilton learned a lot of lessons during his first season and would be even more determined to win the championship the

Drivers' Championship

01.	Kimi Räikkönen	110
02.	Lewis Hamilton	109*
03.	Fernando Alonso	109
04.	Felipe Massa	94
05.	Nick Heidfeld	61
06.	Robert Kubica	39
07.	Heikki Kovalainen	30
08.	Giancarlo Fisichella	21
09.	Nico Rosberg	20
10.	David Coulthard	14
11.	Alexander Wurz	13
12.	Mark Webber	10
13.	Jarno Trulli	8
14.	Sebastian Vettel	6**
15.	Jenson Button	6
16.	Ralf Schumacher	5
17.	Takuma Sato	4
18.	Vitantonio Liuzzi	3
19.	Adrian Sutil	1

*More second places than Fernando Alonso
**More fourth places than Jenson Button

Constructors' Championship

01.	Ferrari	204
02.	BMW	101
03.	Renault	51
04.	Williams-Toyota	33
05.	Red Bull-Renault	24
06.	Toyota	13
07.	Scuderia Toro Rosso-Ferrari	8
08.	Honda	6
09.	Super Aguri-Honda	4
10.	Spyker-Ferrari	1

McLaren-Mercedes were excluded from the Constructors' Championship. Their score of 218 points would have been enough to make them champions.

LEWIS HAMILTON'S JOURNEY TO THE TOP

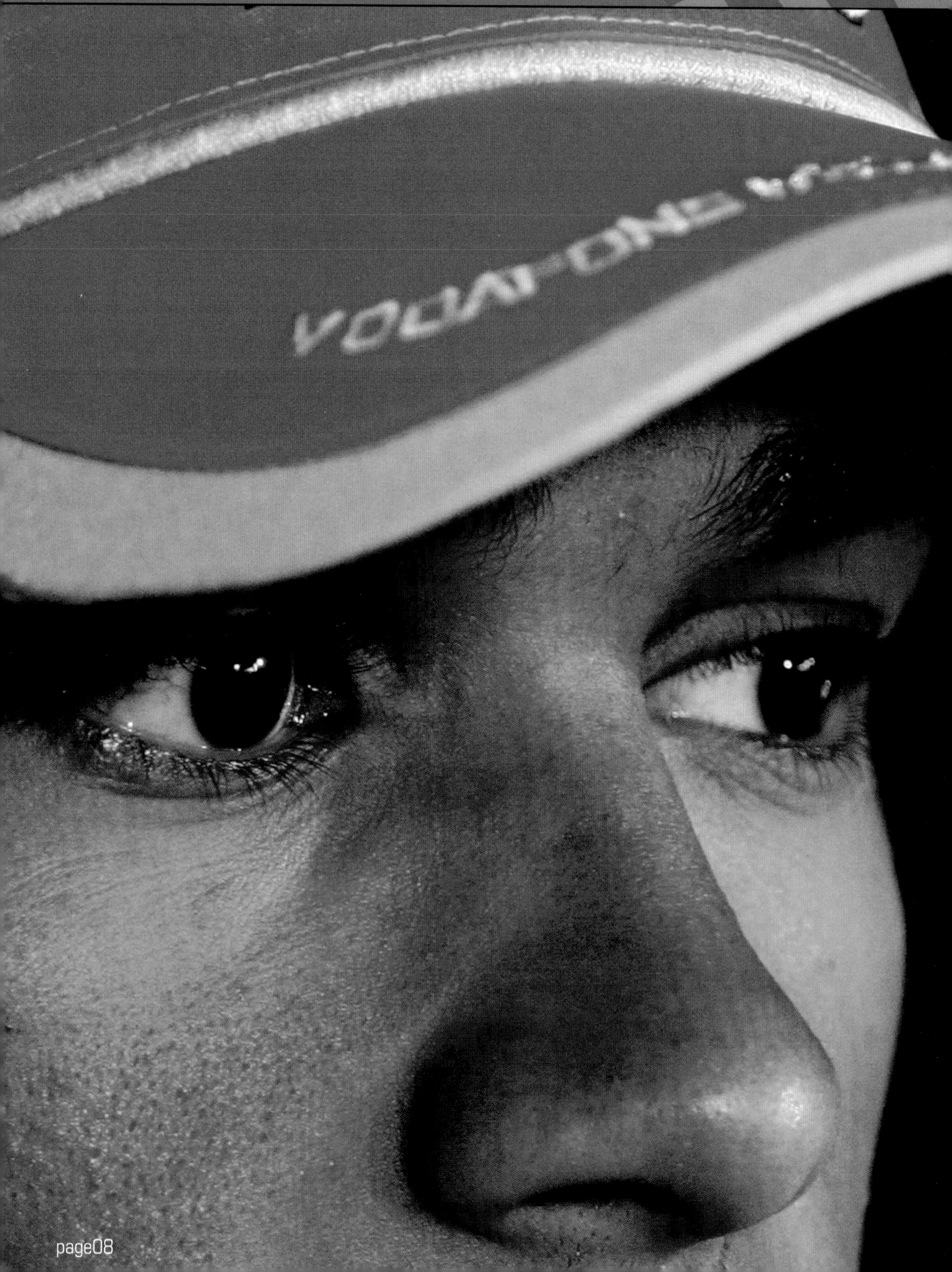

One of the most exciting new drivers in years, Britain's Lewis Hamilton looks set for a fantastic career. He finished second in his rookie season and is hoping to be crowned champion in 2008. This is his journey so far...

In 2001, Lewis finished fifth in the British Formula Renault winter series.

In 2002, Lewis finishes third, with three race wins, in British Formula Renault championship.

In 2003, he won the British Formula Renault championship.

In 2005, he was crowned Formula 3 Euroseries champion.

In 2006, Lewis won the GP2 Series.

In 2006, on September 13th, Lewis was given his first test in a McLaren Formula One car. On 24th November he was confirmed as a race driver for McLaren for the 2007 season.

In 2007, Lewis finished in third at the Australian Grand Prix on his F1 debut and is only the 13th driver to finish on the podium after the first race. He then started on the front row of the Bahrain Grand Prix and finished second to Felipe Massa. Another second place, this time in Spain, saw Lewis take the lead in the Driver's Championship. At the Canadian Grand Prix he started on pole and won his first F1 race. After gearbox problems in the final race of the season, Championship leader Lewis failed to get the necessary points needed to win the title and Kimi Räikkönen dramatically snatched the title by one point.

In 2008, Lewis won the British Grand Prix for the first time at Silverstone – let's hope it's the first of many!

In 1995, he was British cadet class and STP karting champion.

In 1996, he won the 'Champions of the Future', Sky TV KartMasters and Five Nations karting series.

In 1997, Lewis moved up to junior Yamaha and won Champions of the Future series and Super One series.

In 1998, Lewis competed in junior Intercontinental A and was second in McLaren Mercedes Champions of the Future and fourth at the Italian Open. It was confirmed he would be supported by McLaren and Mercedes-Benz.

In 1999, Lewis was crowned Italian 'Industrials' champion at Intercontinental A level. Vice European champion, Trophy de Pomposa winner and fourth at Italian Open Championship at junior-Intercontinental level.

In 2000, he became European Champion at Formula A level and won the World Cup and the Masters at Bercy. Named as British Racing Drivers' Club 'Rising Star' member.

CIRCUIT BREAKER QUIZ

How good is your knowledge of world F1 circuits? Well, you are about to find out! Study the pictures below and try and work out the host country – there are clues if you look hard enough!

Answers on pg 61

DRIVERPROFILES

FERNANDO ALONSO

TEAM: RENAULT
BORN: 29/07/81
NATIONALITY: SPANISH
BIRTHPLACE: OVIEDO, SPAIN
WORLD CHAMPIONSHIPS: 2
HIGHEST FINISH: 1
RACE WINS: 19

SEBASTIEN BOURDAIS

TEAM: TORO ROSSO
BORN: 28/10/79
NATIONALITY: FRENCH
BIRTHPLACE: LE MANS, FRANCE
WORLD CHAMPIONSHIPS: 0
HIGHEST FINISH: 7
RACE WINS: 0

KIMI RÄIKKÖNEN

TEAM: FERRARI
BORN: 17/10/79
NATIONALITY: FINNISH
BIRTHPLACE: ESPOO, FINLAND
WORLD CHAMPIONSHIPS: 1
HIGHEST FINISH: 1
RACE WINS: 17

FELIPE MASSA

TEAM: FERRARI
BORN: 25/4/81
NATIONALITY: BRAZILIAN
BIRTHPLACE: SAO PAULO, BRAZIL
WORLD CHAMPIONSHIPS: 0
HIGHEST FINISH: 1
RACE WINS: 8

DETAILS CORRECT TO 30/07/08

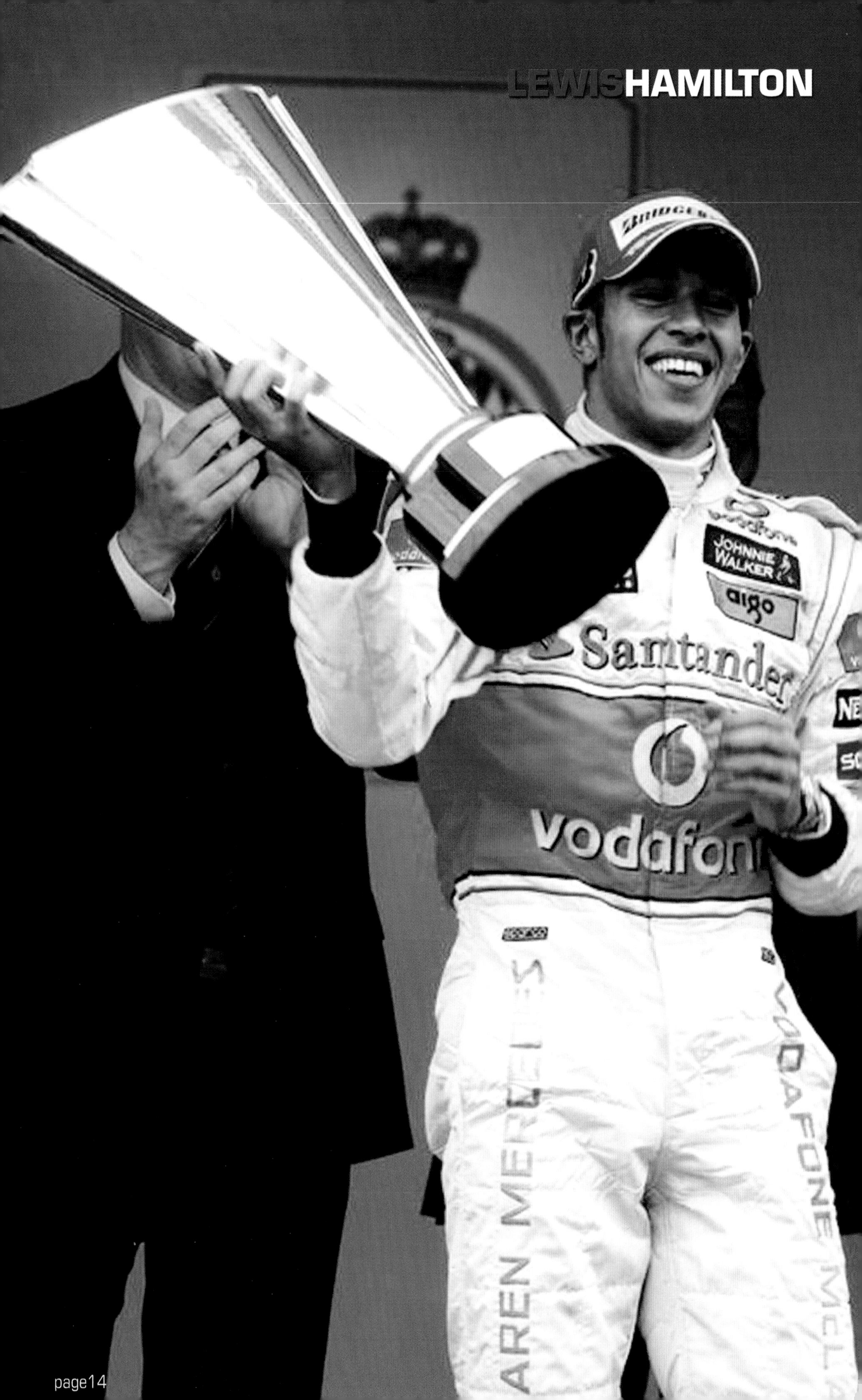
JOHNNIE WALKER
aigo
Santander

SPOT THE DIFFERENCE

Picture A is different from Picture B – can you find and circle the 6 changes we've made in Picture B?

A

B

F1 WORLD CIRCUITS

1

Australian Grand Prix

Albert Park, Melbourne

First Race: 1996
Circuit Length: 5.272 Km
Laps: 58

2

Bahrain Grand Prix

Bahrain International Racing Circuit, Manama

First Race: 2004
Circuit Length: 5.379 Km
Laps: 57

3

Belgian Grand Prix

Spa Francorchamps Circuit

First Race: 1983
(Revised Shorter Version)
Circuit Length: 6.963 Km
Laps: 44

4

Brazilian Grand Prix

Autodromo Jose Carlos Pace, Sao Paulo

First Race: 1973
Circuit Length: 4.283 Km
Laps: 71

SAFETY CAR FACTS

The Safety Car is the unsung hero of Formula One, ensuring drivers' safety during dangerous conditions. Here are some interesting facts about the car that always leads from the front.

The 2008 F1 Safety Car is a Mercedes-Benz, based on the SL 63 AMG model and boasts a 6.3-litre V8 engine with a power output of 386 kW/525 hp and can accelerate from zero to 100 km/h in 4.6 seconds.

The Safety Car is deployed if there is an accident or dangerous weather conditions are threatening to cause major problems. The Race Director (or Clerk of Course) will instruct the marshals to wave yellow flags and hold Safety Car boards aloft to warn drivers the car is now active. From 2007, all F1 drivers had to have LEDs fitted to their steering wheel as an extra warning system that flags are being waved for one reason or another – when the Safety Car is active the LED is illuminated by a yellow light.

The SC was first used at the Canadian Grand Prix in 1973, though it actually caused mayhem by positioning itself in front of the wrong driver, placing several of the cars one lap down and causing considerable headaches for the race organisers who took several hours to figure out who had actually won!

The Safety Car has a green and yellow light bar mounted on its roof – the green light means the driver immediately behind is OK to pass and once the race leader is behind the SC the yellow lights begin to flash.

The SC is operated by a professional driver and has to maintain reasonably fast speeds whilst deployed during a race – this is to ensure the tyres on the racecars remain at operating temperature and the engines don't overheat - Bernd Maylander is the current Safety Car driver for all F1 races.

During the one lap to green, the Safety Car's lights will remain on until it nears the pit lane, when they are switched off – this indicates the race will begin momentarily.

Up to the 2008 season, the 1999 Canadian Grand Prix was the only F1 race to finish behind the Safety Car.

THE BIG F1 QUIZ

Test your knowledge and try and complete the race by answering all 20 questions – then work out your score and see how you did!

1 At which circuit was Kimi Räikkönen crowned the world champion in 2007?
(1 point)

2 The team Fernando Alonso joined after leaving McLaren (2 points)

3 Name the three street circuits used during the 2008 F1 season (3 points)

4 Who has been crowned F1 champion the most? A) Jackie Stewart B) Ayrton Senna C) Michael Schumacher (2 points)

5 If you are shown a black flag, what must you do? (1 point)

6 The total number of races in the 2008 F1 season is...? (2 points)

7 In 2008, Lewis Hamilton won the British Grand Prix for the second time. True or false? (1 point)

8 This current F1 driver has a father who has been crowned world champion three times (3 points)

9 Solve this anagram to discover the name of a current driver: Tick Gloom (1 point)

10 Who were Ferrari's drivers for 2008? (2 points)

11 How many laps did Lewis Hamilton have to complete to win the British Grand Prix at Silverstone? (5 points)

12 Venue for the French Grand Prix (1 point)

13 How many laps is the Monaco Grand Prix? a) 58 b) 68 c) 78   (2 points)

17 These five drivers were all born in Germany – Nelson Piquet Jr, Nico Rosberg, Nick Heidfeld, Sebastian Vettel and Timo Glock. True or false?   (2 points)

14 Venue of Japanese Grand Prix 2008   (2 points)

18 Who is ITV's F1 anchorman? A) Steve Rider B) Murray Hamilton C) Jon Champion   (1 point)

15 Solve this anagram to reveal a race circuit: Gas Pen   (1 point)

19 Can you name the two circuits which share the German Grand Prix?   (2 points)

16 Red Bull's Australian driver for 2008   (2 points)

20 Can you name Force India's 2008 drivers?   (4 points)

Check your answers on pg 61

SCORING: HOW DID YOU DO?

40 points	Climb to the top of the podium – you've won the race in record time!
35-39 points	Fantastic! You've finished on the podium in second place.
30-34 points	Terrific race – you've earned championship points for third position.
25-29 points	Well done – great effort and you've done enough to finish in the points in this race.
20-24 points	You've finished the race but not scored any championship points – well done.
15-19 points	You retired with engine trouble!
14 points or less	Black flag! Return to the pits immediately and start studying F1 again!

DRIVERPROFILES

TAKUMA SATO

TEAM: SUPER AGURI
BORN: 28/1/77
NATIONALITY: JAPANESE
BIRTHPLACE: TOKYO, JAPAN
WORLD CHAMPIONSHIPS: 0
HIGHEST FINISH: 3
RACE WINS: 0

NICO ROSBERG

TEAM: WILLIAMS
BORN: 27/6/85
NATIONALITY: GERMAN
BIRTHPLACE: WIESBADEN, GERMANY
WORLD CHAMPIONSHIPS: 0
HIGHEST FINISH: 3
RACE WINS: 0

KAZUKI NAKAJIMA

TEAM: WILLIAMS
BORN: 11/1/85
NATIONALITY: JAPANESE
BIRTHPLACE: AICHI, JAPAN
WORLD CHAMPIONSHIPS: 0
HIGHEST FINISH: 6
RACE WINS: 0

GIANCARLO FISICHELLA

TEAM: FORCE INDIA
BORN: 14/1/73
NATIONALITY: ITALIAN
BIRTHPLACE: ROME, ITALY
WORLD CHAMPIONSHIPS: 0
HIGHEST FINISH: 1
RACE WINS: 3

DETAILS CORRECT TO 30/07/08

CREATE YOUR OWN
F1 TEAM DESIGN

Get your colouring pens ready and design your own team colours for both car and helmet!

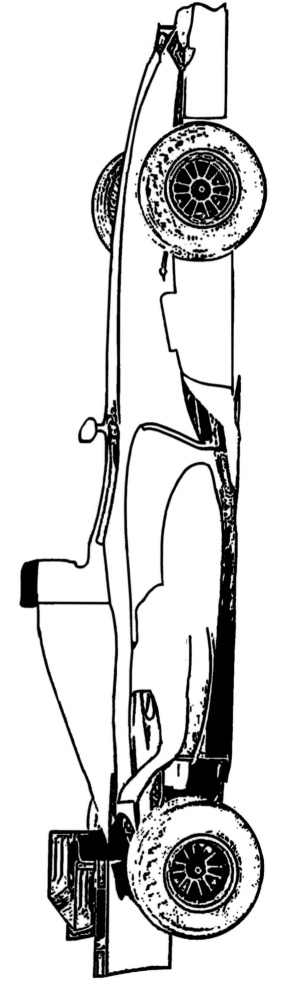

GUESS WHO ?

Can you work out who these four partially disguised drivers are?

Answers on pg 60

F1WORLDCIRCUITS

5

British Grand Prix

Silverstone Circuit

First Race: 1950
Circuit Length: 5.110 Km
Laps: 60

6

Canadian Grand Prix

Circuit Gilles Villeneuve, Montreal

First Race: 1978
Circuit Length: 4.336 Km
Laps: 70

7

Chinese Grand Prix

Shanghai Circuit

First Race: 2004
Circuit Length: 5.419 Km
Laps: 56

8

French Grand Prix

Circuit de Nevers Magny-Cours

First Race: 1991
Circuit Length: 4.386 Km
Laps: 70

F1 CROSSWORD PUZZLE

Read the clues, fill in the relevant spaces and see if you can complete the crossword...

Across

1   David, Scotland's favourite F1 star of recent years (9)
3   A place for refuelling and maintenance (3, 4)
9   The 2006 world champion (8, 6)
13   Every driver would like to stand on this after the race finishes (6)
14   This car is deployed if the race needs to be slowed or stopped (6, 3)
16   The winner sees this flag first (9, 4)
19   The British Grand Prix will be held here in 2010 (9)
20   Cars are weighed in this area (4, 5)

Down

2   A stranded car might need one of these to be taken to safety (3, 5)
4   There are four on each F1 car and they are changed throughout the race (5)
5   The most glamorous street circuit in the world? (6)
6   2009 will be this famous circuit's last appearance for a while (11)
7   You might find this Pole on pole... (6, 6)
8   Where every driver wants to start the race! (4, 8)
10   Nick, the German F1 driver (8)
11   A type of bend (7)
12   Lewis Hamilton's team (7)
15   Felipe Massa's home nation (6)
17   Winners of the 2007 Constructors' Championship (7)
18   A lot of drivers begin in this type of car when they are young (2, 4)

Solution on pg 61

DRIVERPROFILES

MARK WEBBER

TEAM: RED BULL
BORN: 27/8/76
NATIONALITY: AUSTRALIAN
BIRTHPLACE: QUEANBEYAN, AUSTRALIA
WORLD CHAMPIONSHIPS: 0
HIGHEST FINISH: 3
RACE WINS: 0

TIMO GLOCK

TEAM: TOYOTA
BORN: 18/3/82
NATIONALITY: GERMAN
BIRTHPLACE: LINDENFELS, GERMANY
WORLD CHAMPIONSHIPS: 0
HIGHEST FINISH: 4
RACE WINS: 0

RUBENS BARRICHELLO

TEAM: HONDA
BORN: 23/5/72
NATIONALITY: BRAZILIAN
BIRTHPLACE: SAO PAULO, BRAZIL
WORLD CHAMPIONSHIPS: 0
HIGHEST FINISH: 1
RACE WINS: 9

SEBASTIAN VETTEL

TEAM: TORO ROSSO
BORN: 3/7/87
NATIONALITY: GERMAN
BIRTHPLACE: HEPPENHEIM, GERMANY
WORLD CHAMPIONSHIPS: 0
HIGHEST FINISH: 4
RACE WINS: 0

WORDSEARCH

Look at the grid below – can you spot the names of 12 F1 drivers? They can be found upwards, downwards, backwards, forwards or diagonally. Good luck!

```
L X R R K H V M P N P H C D
A C N E N O G C O G M H Y G
C F G P B L V T V C Z D X R
I B B C X B L A Q Z L M O O
B T U H G I E D L E F S P S
U J K T M L D W F A B N L N
K V T A T J J D R E I N R O
Z G H L P O I K R L Y N K L
D T X Q C E N G M X H Q E A
Y N N C H Z H R K Y M Y K N
K O L L E H C I R R A B N B
Y C O U L T H A R D S V R M
J C D R M N N K R L S N P T
K R A I K K O N E N A L R V
```

Answers on pg 61

9

German Grand Prix

Nürburgring Circuit, Nürburg

First Race: 1984
Circuit Length: 5.148
Laps: 60

10

Italian Grand Prix

Autodromo Nazionale Monza, Monza

First Race: 1950
Circuit Length: 5.760 Km
Laps: 53

11

Hungarian Grand Prix

Hungaroring Circuit, Budapest

First Race: 1986
Circuit Length: 4.358 Km
Laps: 70

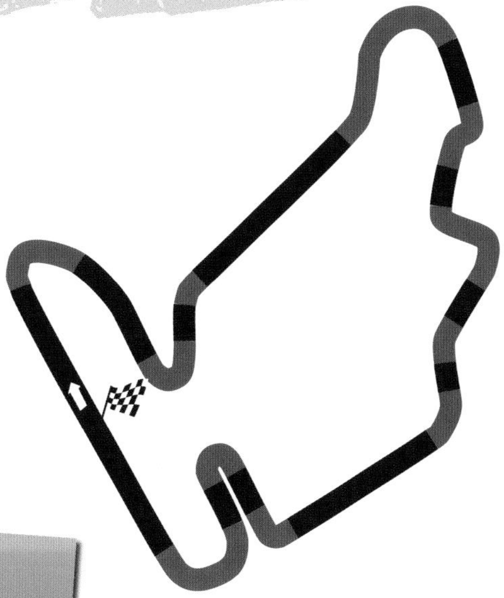

12

Japanese Grand Prix

Fuji Speedway, Oyama

First Race: 1976
Circuit Length: 4.536 Km
Laps: 67

THE A-Z OF F1

Know your lollipop from your bargeboard? Understand the difference between downforce and a slipstream? Here is a look at the various terms and meanings associated with Formula One – from A to Z.

ADR (Accident Data Recorder, "Black Box")

The Accident Data Recorder is similar to an aircraft's black box. It is an electronic component that gathers as much information as possible while the car is in motion to provide clues as to what may have gone wrong in the event of a crash. The ADR must be accessible at all times.

AERODYNAMICS

This is the study of the airflow over and around a Formula 1 car. Designers spend a lot of time ensuring that the latest cars have as little wind resistance as possible.

APEX

The apex is the central point of the inside lane that drivers direct their cars at when turning corners.

APPEAL

F1 teams can make an appeal if they feel their driver has been harshly penalised by race officials.

BALLAST

Ballast is weights that are fixed in specific areas of the cars to achieve the best balance possible for safety reasons. Each F1 car must also be at least equal to the minimum weight requirements.

BAKERSVILLE

This is a huge mobile TV facility that is transported from one race venue to another. Though it sounds as though it is named after a small American town, it is actually named after Bernie Ecclestone's TV chief Eddie Baker.

BARGEBOARD

This is a part of the car body located between the front wheels to help ensure there is a smooth airflow around the side of the car.

BLACK FLAG

Any driver who has a black flag waved at him must go to the pits. A race or qualifying session can also be red-flagged, which means that all drivers must go to the pits.

BLISTERING

A tyre can blister when it becomes too hot. When this happens, parts of the tyre can break away which can happen for various reasons, one of which is the wrong type of tyre for a particular circuit or the tyre pressure being too high.

BLOCKING

Blocking is a similar offence to baulking (when one driver gets in the way of another and slows him down), but it suggests more deliberation. A driver would have to argue his case if accused of blocking and failure to provide a satisfactory explanation could lead to disqualification.

BOTTOMING

This is caused by the chassis of the car hitting the track.

BRAKE BALANCE

There is a switch in the cockpit which drivers can use to switch the brake power from the front to the rear, or vice versa.

CHASSIS

The chassis is the main section of the car – its spine – to which the engine and suspension are attached.

CHICANE

A chicane is a sequence of corners, close together in alternate directions that are often in place to slow cars down before sections of the track that could be dangerous, such as a high-speed corner.

CLEAN AIR

Usually experienced only by the car in front! The air behind the leader and the rest of the cars is turbulent and can affect the aerodynamics needed to achieve the smoothest drive.

COCKPIT

Where the driver sits and the hub of all the car's controls are, located on the chassis.

COMPOUND

The ingredients of a car's tyres, vital to the safety of the driver and specially designed to achieve maximum speed, durability and grip in various weather conditions. A typical F1 car will contain more than 10 different ingredients!

DOWNFORCE

This is the aerodynamic force that pushes down on the car as it travels at speed. Harnessed correctly, this can improve a car's handling, especially around corners.

DRAG

This is the aerodynamic resistance that hits the car as it moves along.

DRIVE-THROUGH-PENALTY

This is one of the two penalties that can be given to drivers during a race. If awarded, the offending driver must drive into the pit lane, continue through without stopping – but adhere to the lane's speed limit – and then rejoin the race.

FLAT SPOT

The part of a tyre affected by a spin or extreme braking. This can ruin the car's handling and often causes the need for a tyre change.

FORMATION LAP

This is a lap involving all the participating cars starting at the grid and finishing at the grid with all cars in their correct starting position for the start of the race.

continued overleaf>>

G-FORCE

A physical force experienced by drivers that can be felt while cornering, accelerating or braking.

GRAINING

Tiny bits of rubber that break away from the tyres and become stuck in the tread.

GRAVEL TRAP

A bed of gravel located on the outside of corners, designed for bringing cars that veer off the track to a safe stop.

GRASS-CUTTING

If a driver leaves the racetrack, his car, more often than not, throws up grass in his wake - this is called grass-cutting.

GURNEY

This is the L-shaped counter flap on the trailing edge of a car's wing.

HAIRPINS

Hairpins are very narrow 180 degree bends, the most famous being the former Loews Hairpin in Monaco, which is now known as the Grand Hotel Hairpin.

HORSEPOWER

This is a somewhat old-fashioned way of measuring engine power outputs. The current F1 engines produce power equal to that of 850 horses!

INSTALLATION LAP

A necessary lap on arrival at a circuit to test functions such as the throttle, steering and brakes before returning to the pits – without crossing the finishing line.

JUMP START

Sensors detect if a driver moves away from his start position before five red lights are showing and if he does, a penalty is imposed.

LOLLIPOP

This is a sign held on a stick in front of a car during a pit stop. It indicates the driver must apply the brakes and engage first gear before the car is lowered off its jacks.

MARSHAL

F1's version of a referee. The marshal's job is to ensure the race runs smoothly and safely and he is also involved in spectator safety, acting as a fire warden when needed, helping to rescue stranded drivers or cars from the track as well as waving flags to signal the track condition to drivers – a busy man!

OVERSTEER

Often a result of turning a corner too quickly, it can be corrected by opposite lock steering by turning the front wheels into a skid.

PADDLES

These are levers located on either side of the rear of the steering wheel enabling the driver to change gear up and down – a sort of F1 gear-stick.

PARC FERME

This is a secure, fenced off area where cars are driven after they've qualified for the race. No team members are allowed to touch the cars, except under the strict supervision of race stewards.

PIT BOARD

This is a board held out on a pit wall, informing a driver of his position in the race as well as how many laps remain.

PIT WALL

This is where the team owner, managers and engineers watch the race, often under some kind of cover to keep rain or bright sunshine off their monitors.

PITS

This is an area separated from the start/finish line by a straight wall. Cars enter the pits during a race for general maintenance such as refuelling or tyre changes.

PLANK

A hard wooden strip fitted underneath all the F1 cars to indicate whether or not the car is being driven too low to the track surface – if the wood shows excessive damage, the problem needs to be rectified.

PODIUM

This, of course, is the wooden dais on which the drivers who finish first, second and third stand at the end of the race and is therefore a much coveted place to be.

POLE POSITION

The aim of every driver and the first position on the starting grid awarded to the driver with the fastest lap recorded during qualification.

QUALIFYING

A knock-out session held on a Saturday where the drivers compete for the best times to decide where they will start on the grid.

RETIREMENT

A driver is forced to retire from a race if his car suffers an irreversible mechanical failure or is involved in an accident.

SAFETY CAR

This is a course vehicle that is called from the pits and drives in

front of the leading car in the event of an incident that means the cars need to be slowed down to a safe speed.

SIDEPOD

Part of the car housing radiators which runs alongside the driver and to the rear wing.

SLIPSTREAMING

This is a tactic used by a driver whereby he catches the car in front, tucks in behind his rear wing therefore reducing the drag over the trailing car's body and opening the possibility of jettisoning past before the next corner.

SPLASH AND DASH

This is a pit stop taken by a car approaching the final few laps of the race whereby the driver requires just a few litres of fuel to complete the course.

STOP-GO PENALTY

A penalty in which a driver must return to his pit and stop for 10 seconds with no refuelling or tyre changes.

TELEMETRY

This is a system that beams information relating to the car's engine and chassis to computers in the pit-garage and enables engineers to monitor the car's

performance.

TORQUE

The turning or twisting force of an engine generally used to measure an engine's flexibility. A powerful engine with little torque may actually be slower than a lesser engine with more torque on certain circuits – achieving the correct balance between the two is essential for a car to achieve continually good results.

TRACTION

This is the degree that a car is able to transfer power onto the track surface for forward momentum.

TYRE WARMER

This is, in effect, an electric blanket to keep tyres close to their optimum operating temperature prior to being fitted.

UNDERSTEER

This occurs when the front end of the car resists turning into a corner and slides wide as the driver attempts to turn towards the apex.

WARM-UP

This is the lap used by drivers to make sure the car is ready to perform at its maximum levels. There is a warm-up session on the Sunday morning before each race.

DRIVERPROFILES

ADRIAN SUTIL

TEAM: FORCE INDIA
BORN: 11/1/83
NATIONALITY: GERMAN
BIRTHPLACE: STARNBERG, GERMANY
WORLD CHAMPIONSHIPS: 0
HIGHEST FINISH: 8
RACE WINS: 0

NICK HEIDFELD

TEAM: BMW SAUBER
BORN: 10/5/77
NATIONALITY: GERMAN
BIRTHPLACE: MONCHENGLADBACH, GERMANY
WORLD CHAMPIONSHIPS: 0
HIGHEST FINISH: 2
RACE WINS: 0

ANTHONY DAVIDSON

TEAM: SUPER AGURI
BORN: 18/4/79
NATIONALITY: ENGLISH
BIRTHPLACE: HEMEL HEMPSTEAD, ENGLAND
WORLD CHAMPIONSHIPS: 0
HIGHEST FINISH: 11
RACE WINS: 0

HEIKKI KOVALAINEN

TEAM: MCLAREN
BORN: 19/10/81
NATIONALITY: FINNISH
BIRTHPLACE: SUOMUSSALMI, FINLAND
WORLD CHAMPIONSHIPS: 0
HIGHEST FINISH: 2
RACE WINS: 0

DETAILS CORRECT TO 30/07/08

SPOT THE DIFFERENCE

Picture A is different from Picture B – can you find and circle the 6 changes we've made in Picture B?

Answers on pg 60

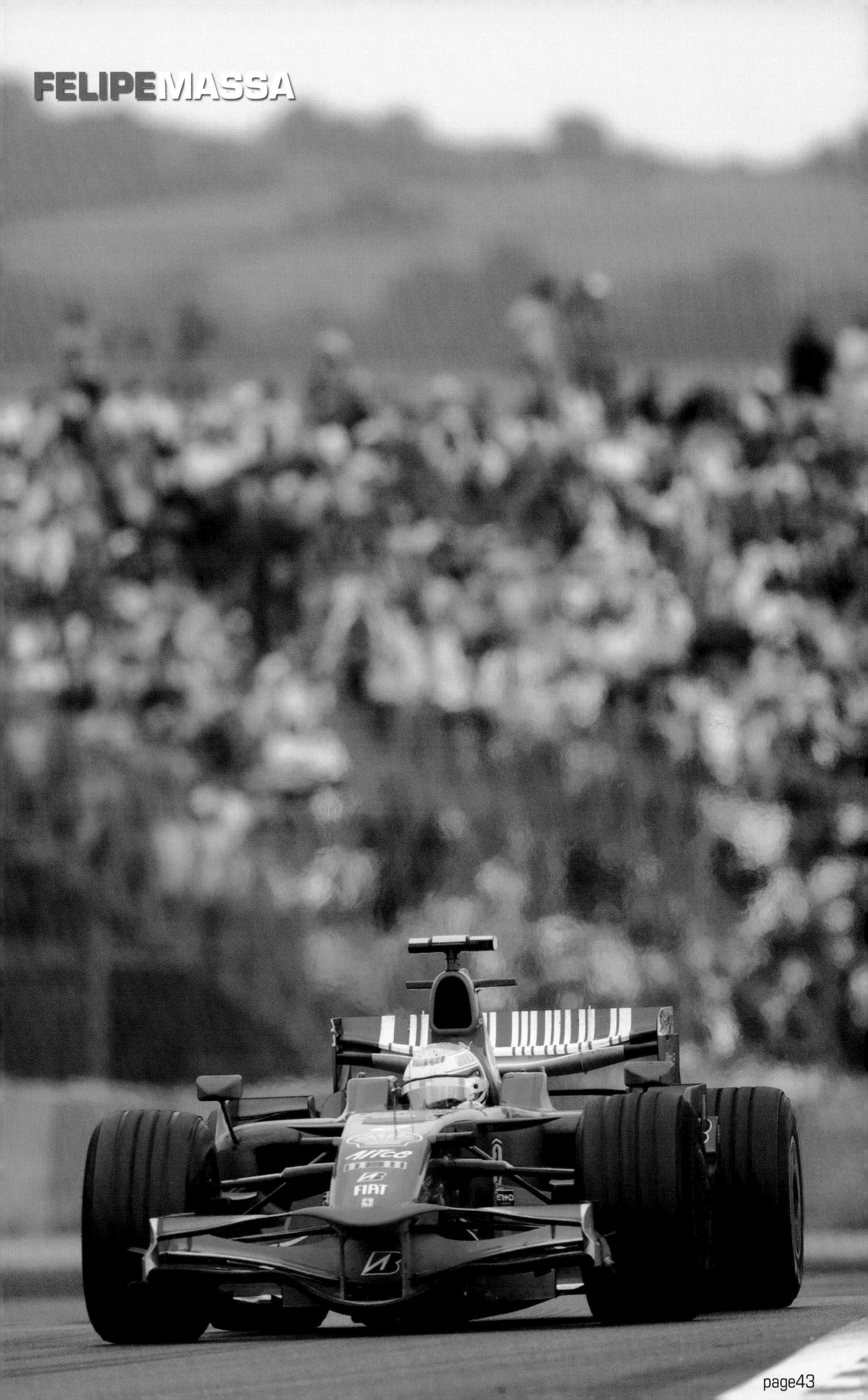
FIAT

13

Malaysian Grand Prix

Sepang International Circuit, Kuala Lumpur

First Race: 1999
Circuit Length: 5.350 Km
Laps: 56

14

Monaco Grand Prix

Street Circuit, Monte Carlo

First Race: 1950
Circuit Length: 3.347 Km
Laps: 78

15

Spanish Grand Prix

Circuit de Catalunya, Barcelona

First Race: 1991
Circuit Length: 4.629 Km
Laps: 66

16

Turkish Grand Prix

Istanbul Park Circuit, Istanbul

First Race: 2005
Circuit Length: 5.344 Km
Laps: 58

F1 DRIVERS & TEAM COLOURS 2008:

Jarno Trulli
(Toyota)

Timo Glock
(Toyota)

Mark Webber
(Red Bull)

Sebastien Bourdais
(Toro Rosso)

Sebastian Vettel
(Toro Rosso)

Takuma Sato
(Super Aguri)

Anthony Davidson
(Super Aguri)

Nick Heidfeld (BMW)   Robert Kubica (BMW)   Felipe Massa (Ferrari)   Kimi Räikkönen
(Ferrari)

David Coulthard
(Red Bull)

Jenson Button
(Honda)

Rubens Barrichello
(Honda)

Giancarlo
Fisichella
(Force India)

Adrian Sutil
(Force India)

Nico Rosberg
(Williams)

Kazuki Nakajima
(Williams)

ING
AUSTRALIAN
GRAND PRIX
MELBOURNE 2008

Lewis Hamilton
(McLaren)

Heikki Kovalainen
(McLaren)

Fernando Alonso
(Renault)

Nelsinho Piquet
(Renault)

KNOW YOUR FLAGS!

Whether you're a spectator, race official or - most importantly - a driver, knowing the flags of Formula One is vital and could even save lives. Of course, all drivers have to learn the colours of the 10 F1 flags before they begin driving and also understand why they are waved during the race. Here is a guide to each flag - its colour and what it means - so by the time you next watch a Grand Prix, you'll know exactly what is happening!

CHEQUERED FLAG

when the chequered flag is waved, the race has ended. Perhaps the most famous flag in world sport, the first person to see it is the winner – then it is waved to each car that crosses the line behind them.

RED FLAG

The waving of the red flag means only one thing – the race has been stopped. The reasons for this will be either because of an accident, a car has come to a halt in a dangerous position or conditions are too severe to continue.

YELLOW FLAG

A yellow flag indicates there is danger ahead and therefore no overtaking is allowed. A single yellow flag means drivers must slow down and a double yellow flag warns drivers that they must be prepared to stop if necessary.

BLUE FLAG

This is shown to a particular driver to inform them that a faster car is behind him and trying to overtake. A car that has been lapped must allow the faster car past after seeing a maximum of three blue flags – if he still doesn't allow room to be overtaken, he may well be penalised. A car that is racing and has not been lapped is under no obligation to move over.

BLACK FLAG
If a driver sees this flag it usually means his race is over. It means 'head to the pits immediately.' It is waved if rules have been broken and often precedes disqualification.

RED AND YELLOW STRIPED FLAG
This means the circuit is slippery, most often due to oil or excessive water on the track.

GREEN FLAG
When the green flag is waved it means that a hazard has been cleared up and drivers can now continue at normal racing speed.

BLACK FLAG WITH AN ORANGE DISC
This will be shown only to an individual driver to indicate he has a mechanical problem and therefore must return to his pit immediately.

WHITE AND BLACK DIAGONAL HALVES
Not a flag that is overly used, this will be shown – along with the targeted car number – to a driver that he has been judged to have behaved in an unsporting manner. If he ignores this, a black flag may follow, ending his race.

WHITE FLAG
A white flag indicates there is a slow-moving vehicle on the track – possibly the safety car or a tow truck.

F1 HALL OF FAME

Here is a gallery of winners from the past 30 years...

When Kimi Räikkönen was dramatically crowned the 2007 F1 world champion last season, he became the 29th driver in 57 years to win the title. Only a select few have won the title more than once and only a handful of gifted men have won the championship more than twice.

Arguments rage as to who is the greatest F1 driver of all time, but nobody could argue that Michael Schumacher wasn't the most successful with an astonishing seven titles to his name. Juan Manuel Fangio secured five titles during the 1950s, Alain Prost won four championships in total and Ayrton Senna, Nelson Piquet, Niki Lauda, Jackie Stewart

and Jack Brabham won three each.

The very first Formula One winner was Italian Nino Farina, whose stylish driving techniques saw him clinch the 1950 championship and Argentine Juan Manuel Fangio took the trophy the following year before Alberto Ascari won in successive years to bring the title back to Italy. Fangio, who many consider to be the greatest driver of all-time, then dominated Formula One for four years before Britain celebrated its first success, with the larger-than-life Mike Hawthorn winning in 1958 – his only title. Next to be crowned best driver of the year was Australian Jack Brabham who won two successive titles

1978 MARIO ANDRETTI

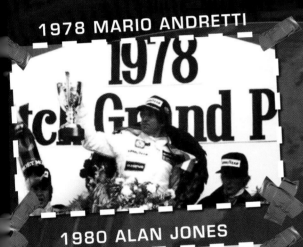

1979 JODY SCHECKTER

1980 ALAN JONES

1981 NELSON PIQUET

1982 KEKE ROSBERG

1983 NELSON PIQUET

by America's Phil Hill, a gifted driver who, despite his success, never really embraced the sport – certainly not as wholeheartedly as Britain's Graham Hill who won the first of his two championships in 1962.

As the years went on, other notable champions emerged over the years and each decade had its superstars. In the Seventies,

Lauda were the golden boys of F1 – each would win the title three times during their career and Brazilian Nelson Piquet and French genius Alain Prost took three titles apiece during the 1980s.

At the end of the decade, it was perhaps the most enigmatic driver of all time who took control of F1 – Brazil's magnificent Ayrton Senna. Stylish, brilliant behind the wheel and continued overleaf>>

1984 NIKI LAUDA

1985 ALAIN PROST

1986 ALAIN PROST

1987 NELSON PIQUET

1988 AYRTON SENNA

1989 ALAIN PROST

1990 AYRTON SENNA

1991 AYRTON SENNA

F1 HALL OF FAME

continually pushing back the boundaries of the sport, he was a superstar with a legion of admirers. He died when his car spectacularly crashed into a concrete wall during the 1994 San Marino Grand Prix and the world of Formula One was a much duller place without the mercurial Senna.

Though there were further successes for Britain along the way, most notably for Nigel Mansell in 1992 and Damon Hill, son of double champion Graham Hill, clinched the championship in 1996. Finland's Mika Häkkinen's double success in 1998 and 1999 was sandwiched in-between the incredible domination of F1 by Germany's Michael Schumacher.

The ruthless German won his first back-to-back titles in 1994 and 1995, but it was at the turn of the century that his talent really shone, winning five consecutive titles between 2000 and 2004 to become the most successful driver ever, winning an amazing total of 91 Grand Prix races.

It's hard to see that record ever being surpassed; though the likes of Fernando Alonso and Lewis Hamilton will be doing everything they can to emulate Schumacher's fantastic record. Are they capable or is there a new kid on the block waiting to burst through? Only time will tell! Here is a gallery of winners for the past 30 years...

1992 NIGEL MANSELL

1993 ALAIN PROST

1994 MICHAEL SCHUMACHER

1995 MICHAEL SCHUMACHER

1996 DAMON HILL

1997 JACQUES VILLENEUVE

2000 MICHAEL SCHUMACHER

2001 MICHAEL SCHUMACHER

2002 MICHAEL SCHUMACHER

2003 MICHAEL SCHUMACHER

2004 MICHAEL SCHUMACHER

2005 FERNANDO ALONSO

2006 FERNANDO ALONSO

2007 KIMI RAIKKONEN

DRIVERPROFILES

DAVID COULTHARD

TEAM: RED BULL
BORN: 27/03/71
NATIONALITY: SCOTTISH
BIRTHPLACE: TWYNHOLM, SCOTLAND
WORLD CHAMPIONSHIPS: 0
HIGHEST FINISH: 1
RACE WINS: 13

JENSON BUTTON

TEAM: HONDA
BORN: 19/1/80
NATIONALITY: ENGLISH
BIRTHPLACE: FROME, ENGLAND
WORLD CHAMPIONSHIPS: 0
HIGHEST FINISH: 1
RACE WINS: 1

NELSINHO PIQUET

TEAM: RENAULT
BORN: 25/7/85
NATIONALITY: BRAZILIAN
BIRTHPLACE: HEIDELBERG, GERMANY
WORLD CHAMPIONSHIPS: 0
HIGHEST FINISH: 2
RACE WINS: 0

LEWIS HAMILTON

TEAM: MCLAREN
BORN: 7/1/85
NATIONALITY: ENGLISH
BIRTHPLACE: STEVENAGE, ENGLAND
WORLD CHAMPIONSHIPS: 0
HIGHEST FINISH: 1
RACE WINS: 8

DETAILS CORRECT TO 30/07/08

WHERE FROM THE AIR ?

There are four _F1_ circuits here viewed from a lofty position, can you name them all?

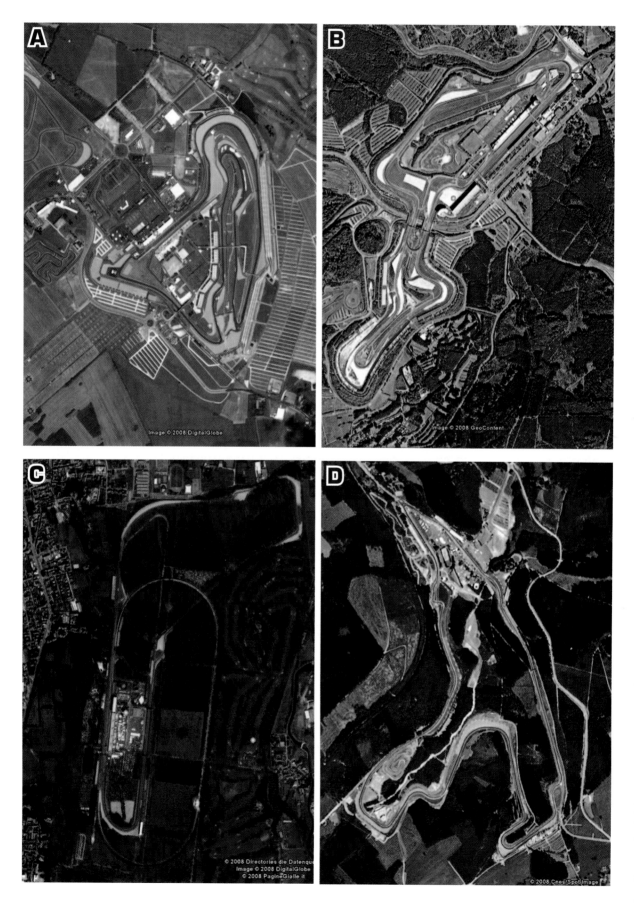

Answers on pg 60

KIMI RÄIKKÖNEN

F1 **WORLD**CIRCUITS

Singapore

Street Circuit, Singapore

First Race: 2008
Circuit Length: 5.037 Km
Laps: 61

European Grand Prix (Spain)

Street Circuit, Valencia

First Race: 2008
Circuit Length: 5.442 Km
Laps: 57

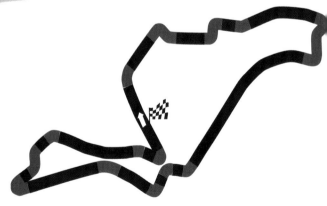

DRIVER PROFILES

JARNO TRULLI

TEAM: TOYOTA
BORN: 13/7/74
NATIONALITY: ITALIAN
BIRTHPLACE: PESCARA, ITALY
WORLD CHAMPIONSHIPS: 0
HIGHEST FINISH: 1
RACE WINS: 1

ROBERT KUBICA

TEAM: BMW SAUBER
BORN: 7/12/84
NATIONALITY: POLISH
BIRTHPLACE: KRAKOW, POLAND
WORLD CHAMPIONSHIPS: 0
HIGHEST FINISH: 1
RACE WINS: 1

DETAILS CORRECT TO 30/07/08

QUIZANSWERS

WHERE FROM THE AIR? ANSWERS (PG 56)

A, Magny-Cours, France
B, Nurburg, Germany

C, Monza, Italy
D, Spa Francorchamps, Belgium

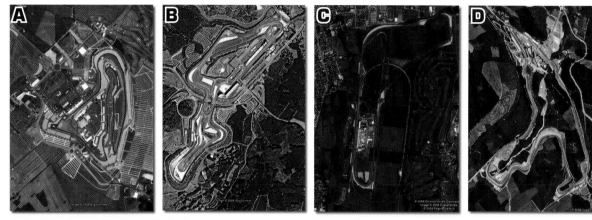

SPOT THE DIFFERENCE ANSWERS (PG 42)
Did you find all six changes in Picture B?

SPOT THE DIFFERENCE ANSWERS (PG 15)
Did you find all six changes in Picture B?

GUESS WHO?
ANSWERS (PG 25)
Did you figure out who the drivers were?

A) NICK HEIDFELD

B) FELIPE MASSA

C) FERNANDO ALONSO

D) JARNO TRULLI

L	X	R	R	K	H	V	M	P	N	P	H	C	D
A	C	N	E	N	O	G	C	O	G	M	H	Y	G
C	F	G	P	B	L	V	T	V	C	Z	D	X	R
I	B	B	C	X	B	L	A	Q	Z	L	M	O	O
B	T	U	H	G	I	E	D	L	E	F	S	P	S
U	J	K	T	M	L	D	W	F	A	B	N	L	N
K	V	T	A	T	J	J	D	R	E	I	N	R	O
Z	G	H	L	P	O	I	K	R	L	Y	N	K	L
D	T	X	Q	C	E	N	G	M	X	H	Q	E	A
Y	N	N	C	H	Z	H	R	K	Y	M	Y	K	N
K	O	L	L	E	H	C	I	R	R	A	B	N	B
Y	C	O	U	L	T	H	A	R	D	S	V	R	M
J	C	D	R	M	N	N	K	R	L	S	N	P	T
K	R	A	I	K	K	O	N	E	N	A	L	R	V

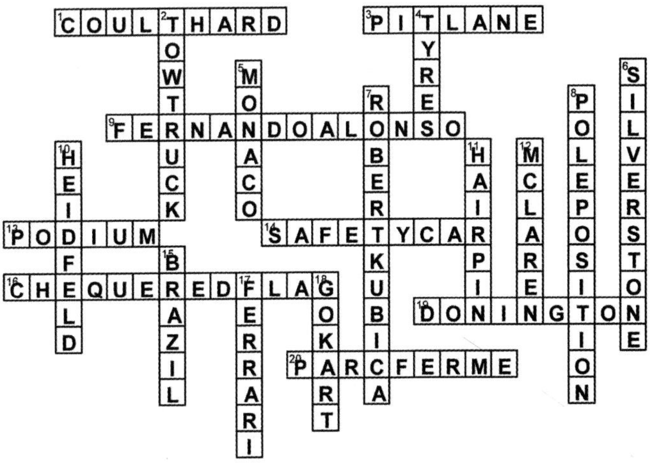

1 COULTHARD
2 TOWTRUCK
3 PITLANE
4 TYRES
5 MONACO
6 SILVERSTONE
7 ROBERTKUBICA
8 POLEPOSITION
9 FERNANDOALONSO
10 HEIDFELD
11 HAIRPIN
12 MCLAREN
13 PODIUM
14 SAFETYCAR
15 BRAZIL
16 CHEQUEREDFLAG
17 FERRARI
18 GOKART
19 DONINGTON
20 PARCFERME

WORDSEARCH SOLUTION (PG 32)

CROSSWORD SOLUTION (PG 28)

THE**BIG** F1 QUIZ

ANSWERS FROM (PGS 20&21)

01	BRAZIL
02	RENAULT
03	VALENCIA, MONACO AND SINGAPORE
04	C) MICHAEL SCHUMACHER
05	RETURN TO THE PITS IMMEDIATELY
06	17
07	FALSE – IT WAS HIS FIRST WIN ON HOME SOIL
08	NELSON PIQUET JR
09	TIMO GLOCK
10	FELIPE MASSA AND KIMI RAIKKONEN
11	60
12	MAGNY-COURS
13	C) 78
14	FUJI SPEEDWAY
15	SEPANG
16	MARK WEBBER
17	TRUE
18	A) STEVE RIDER
19	NÜRBURGRING AND HOCKENHEIM
20	ADRIAN SUTIL AND GIANCARLO FISICHELLA

CIRCUIT BREAKER QUIZ ANSWERS (PGS 10&11)

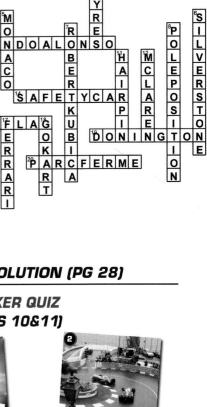

1
1 MOROCCO

2
2 MONACO

3
3 SILVERSTONE, UK

4
4 FRANCE

5
5 CANADA

6
6 TURKEY

7
7 SPAIN

8
8 BAHRAIN

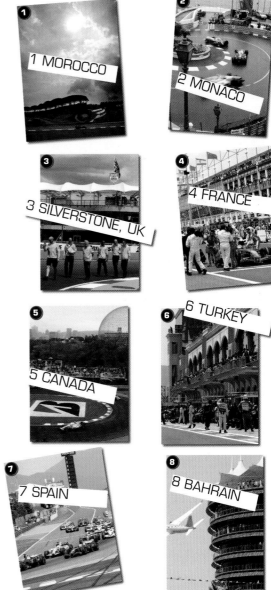